The Giaour

By Lord Byron

A Fragment of a Turkish Tale

No breath of air to break the wave
That rolls below the Athenian's grave,
That tomb which, gleaming o'er the cliff
First greets the homeward-veering skiff
High o'er the land he saved in vain;
When shall such Hero live again?

Fair clime! where every season smiles
  Benignant o'er those blesséd isles,
  Which, seen from far Colonna's height,
  Make glad the heart that hails the sight,
  And lend to lonliness delight.
  There mildly dimpling, Ocean's cheek
  Reflects the tints of many a peak
  Caught by the laughing tides that lave
  These Edens of the Eastern wave:
  And if at times a transient breeze
  Break the blue crystal of the seas,
  Or sweep one blossom from the trees,
  How welcome is each gentle air
  That waves and wafts the odours there!
  For there the Rose, o'er crag or vale,
  Sultana of the Nightingale,

  The maid for whom his melody,
  His thousand songs are heard on high,
  Blooms blushing to her lover's tale:
  His queen, the garden queen, his Rose,
  Unbent by winds, unchilled by snows,
  Far from winters of the west,
  By every breeze and season blest,
  Returns the sweets by Nature given
  In soft incense back to Heaven;
  And gratefu yields that smiling sky

Her fairest hue and fragrant sigh.
And many a summer flower is there,
And many a shade that Love might share,
And many a grotto, meant by rest,
That holds the pirate for a guest;
Whose bark in sheltering cove below
Lurks for the pasiing peaceful prow,
Till the gay mariner's guitar
Is heard, and seen the Evening Star;

Then stealing with the muffled oar,
Far shaded by the rocky shore,
Rush the night-prowlers on the prey,
And turns to groan his roudelay.
Strange—that where Nature loved to trace,
As if for Gods, a dwelling place,
And every charm and grace hath mixed
Within the Paradise she fixed,
There man, enarmoured of distress,
Should mar it into wilderness,
And trample, brute-like, o'er each flower
That tasks not one labourious hour;
Nor claims the culture of his hand
To blood along the fairy land,
But springs as to preclude his care,
And sweetly woos him—but to spare!
Strange—that where all is Peace beside,
There Passion riots in her pride,
And Lust and Rapine wildly reign
To darken o'er the fair domain.
It is as though the Fiends prevailed
Against the Seraphs they assailed,
And, fixed on heavenly thrones, should dwell
The freed inheritors of Hell;

So soft the scene, so formed for joy,
So curst the tyrants that destroy!

He who hath bent him o'er the dead
Ere the first day of Death is fled,
The first dark day of Nothingness,
The last of Danger and Distress,
(Before Decay's effacing fingers
Have swept the lines where Beauty lingers,)
And marked the mild angelic air,
The rapture of Repose that's there,
The fixed yet tender thraits that streak
The languor of the placid cheek,
And—but for that sad shrouded eye,
That fires not, wins not, weeps not, now,
And but for that chill, changeless brow,

Where cold Obstruction's apathy
Appals the gazing mourner's heart,
As if to him it could impart
The doom he dreads, yet dwells upon;
Yes, but for these and these alone,
Some moments, aye, one treacherous hour,
He still might doubt the Tyrant's power;
So fair, so calm, so softly sealed,
The first, last look by Death revealed!
Such is the aspect of his shore;
'T is Greece, but living Greece no more!
So coldly sweet, so deadly fair,
We start, for Soul is wanting there.
Hers is the loveliness in death,
That parts not quite with parting breath;
But beauty with that fearful bloom,
That hue which haunts it to the tomb,

Expression's last receding ray,
A gilded Halo hovering round decay,
The farewell beam of Feeling past away!
Spark of that flame, perchance of heavenly birth,
Which gleams, but warms no more its cherished earth!

Clime of the unforgotten brave!
Whose land from plain to mountain-cave
Was Freedom;s home or Glory's grave!
Shrine of the mighty! can it be,
That this is all remains of thee?
Approach, thou craven crouching slave:
Say, is this not Thermopylæ?
These waters blue that round you lave,—
Of servile offspring of the free—
Pronounce what sea, what shore is this?
The gulf, the rock of Salamis!
These scenes, their story yet unknown;
Arise, and make again your own;
Snatch from the ashes of your Sires
The embers of their former fires;
And he who in the strife expires
Will add to theirs a name of fear
That Tyranny shall quake to hear,
And leave his sons a hope, a fame,
They too will rather die than shame:
For Freedom's battle once begun,
Bequeathed by bleeding Sire to Son,
Though baffled oft is ever won.
Bear witness, Greece, thy living page!
Attest it many a deathless age!
While Kings, in dusty darkness hid,
Have left a nameless pyramid,
Thy Heroes, though the general doom

Hath swept the column from their tomb,
A mightier monument command,
The mountains of thy native land!
There points thy Muse to stranger's eye
The graves of those that cannot die!
'T were long to tell, and sad to trace,
Each step from Spledour to Disgrace;
Enough—no foreign foe could quell
Thy soul, till from itself it fell;
Yet! Self-abasement paved the way
To villain-bonds and despot sway.

What can he tell who tread thy shore?
No legend of thine olden time,
No theme on which the Muse might soar
High as thine own days of yore,
When man was worthy of thy clime.
The hearts within thy valleys bred,
The fiery souls that might have led
Thy sons to deeds sublime,
Now crawl from cradle to the Grave,
Slaves—nay, the bondsmen of a Slave,
And callous, save to crime.
Stained with each evil that pollutes
Mankind, where least above the brutes;
Without even savage virtue blest,
Without one free or valiant breast,
Still to the neighbouring ports tey waft
Proverbial wiles, and ancient craft;
In this subtle Greek is found,
For this, and this alown, renowned.
In vain might Liberty invoke
The spirit to its bondage broke
Or raise the neck that courts the yoke:

No more her sorrows I bewail,

Yet this will be a mournful tale,
And they who listen may believe,
Who heard it first had cause to grieve.

Far, dark, along the blue sea glancing,
The shadows of the rocks advancing
Start on the fisher's eye like boat
Of island-pirate or Mainote;
And fearful for his light caïque,
He shuns the near but doubtful creek:
Though worn and weary with his toil,
And cumbered with his scaly spoil,
Slowly, yet strongly, plies the oar,
Till Port Leone's safer shore
Receives him by the lovely light
That best becomes an Eastern night.

... Who thundering comes on blackest steed,
With slackened bit and hoof of speed?
Beneath the clattering iron's sound
The caverned echoes wake around
In lash for lash, and bound for bound;
The foam that streaks the courser's side
Seems gathered from the ocean-tide:
Though weary waves are sunk to rest,
There's none within his rider's breast;
And though tomorrow's tempest lower,
'Tis calmer than thy heart, young Giaour!
I know thee not, I loathe thy race,
But in thy lineaments I trace
What time shall strengthen, not efface:
Though young and pale, that sallow front

Is scathed by fiery passion's brunt;
Though bent on earth thine evil eye,
As meteor-like thou glidest by,
Right well I view thee and deem thee one
Whom Othman's sons should slay or shun.

On - on he hastened, and he drew
My gaze of wonder as he flew:
Though like a demon of the night
He passed, and vanished from my sight,
His aspect and his air impressed
A troubled memory on my breast,
And long upon my startled ear
Rung his dark courser's hoofs of fear.
He spurs his steed; he nears the steep,
That, jutting, shadows o'er the deep;
He winds around; he hurries by;
The rock relieves him from mine eye;
For, well I ween, unwelcome he
Whose glance is fixed on those that flee;
And not a start that shines too bright
On him who takes such timeless flight.
He wound along; but ere he passed
One glance he snatched, as if his last,
A moment checked his wheeling steed,
A moment breathed him from his speed,
A moment on his stirrup stood -
Why looks he o'er the olive wood?
The crescent glimmers on the hill,
The mosque's high lamps are quivering still
Though too remote for sound to wake
In echoes of far tophaike,
The flashes of each joyous peal

Are seen to prove the Moslem's zeal,
Tonight, set Rhamazani's sun;
Tonight the Bairam feast's begun;
Tonight - but who and what art thou
Of foreign garb and fearful brow?
That thou should'st either pause or flee?

He stood - some dread was on his face,
Soon hatred settled in its place:
It rose not with the reddening flush
Of transient anger's hasty blush,
But pale as marble o'er the tomb,
Whose ghastly whiteness aids its gloom.
His brow was bent, his eye was glazed;
He raised his arm, and fiercely raised,
And sternly shook his hand on high,
As doubting to return or fly;
Impatient of his flight delayed,
Here loud his raven charger neighed -
Down glanced that hand and, and grasped his blade;
That sound had burst his waking dream,
As slumber starts at owlet's scream.
The spur hath lanced his courser's sides;
Away, away, for life he rides:
Swift as the hurled on high jerreed
Springs to the touch his startled steed;
The rock is doubled, and the shore
Shakes with the clattering tramp no more;
The crag is won, no more is seen
His Christian crest and haughty mien.
'Twas but an instant he restrained
That fiery barb so sternly reined;
'Twas but a moment that he stood,
Then sped as if by death pursued;

But in that instant o'er his soul
Winters of memory seemed to roll,
And gather in that drop of time
A life of pain, an age of crime.
O'er him who loves, or hates, or fears,
Such moment pours the grief of years:
What felt he then, at once opprest
By all that most distracts the breast?
That pause, which pondered o'er his fate,
Oh, who its dreary length shall date!
Though in time's record nearly nought,
It was eternity to thought!
For infinite as boundless space
The thought that conscience must embrace,
Which in itself can comprehend
Woe without name, or hope, or end.

The hour is past, the Giaour is gone;
And did he fly or fall alone?
Woe to that hour he came or went!
The curse for Hassan's sin was sent
To turn a palace to a tomb:
He came, he went, like the Simoom,
That harbinger of fate and gloom,
Beneath whose widely - wasting breath
The very cypress droops to death -
Dark tree, still sad when others' grief is fled,
The only constant mourner o'er the dead!

The steed is vanished from the stall;
No serf is seen in Hassan's hall;
The lonely spider's thin grey pall
Waves slowly widening o'er the wall;
The bat builds in his harem bower,

And in the fortress of his power
The owl usurps the beacon-tower;
The wild-dog howls o'er the fountain's brim,
With baffled thirst and famine, grim;
For the stream has shrunk from its marble bed,
Where the weeds and the desolate dust are spread.
'Twas sweet of yore to see it play
And chase the sultriness of day,
As springing high the silver dew
In whirls fantastically flew,
And flung luxurious coolness round
The air, and verdure o'er the ground.
'Twas sweet, when cloudless stars were bright,
To view the wave of watery light,
And hear its melody by night.
And oft had Hassan's childhood played
Around the verge of that cascade;
And oft upon his mother's breast
That sound had harmonized his rest;
And oft had Hassan's youth along
Its bank been soothed by beauty's song;
And softer seem'd each melting tone
Of music mingled with its own.
But ne'er shall Hassan's age repose
Along the brink at twilight's close:
The stream that filled that font is fled -
The blood that warmed his heart is shed!
And here no more shall human voice
Be heard to rage, regret, rejoice.
The last sad note that swelled the gale
Was woman's wildest funeral wall:
That quenched in silence all is still,
But the lattice that flaps when the wind is shrill:
Though raves the gust, and floods the rain,

No hand shall clasp its clasp again.
On desert sands 'twere joy to scan
The rudest steps of fellow man,
So here the very voice of grief
Might wake an echo like relief -
At least 'twould say, 'All are not gone;
There lingers life, though but in one' -
For many a gilded chamber's there,
Which solitude might well forbear;
Within that dome as yet decay
Hath slowly worked her cankering way -
But gloom is gathered o'er the gate,
Nor there the fakir's self will wait;
Nor there will wandering dervise stay,
For bounty cheers not his delay;
Nor there will weary stranger halt
To bless the sacred 'bread and salt'.
Alike must wealth and poverty
Pass heedless and unheeded by,
For courtesy and pity died
With Hassan on the mountain side.
His roof, that refuge unto men,
Is desolation's hungry den.
The guest flies the hall, and the vassal from labour,
Since his turban was cleft by the infidel's sabre!

I hear the sound of coming feet,
But not a voice mine ear to greet;
More near - each turban I can scan,
And silver-sheathed ataghan;
The foremost of the band is seen
An emir by his garb of green:
 'Ho! Who art thou?' - 'This low salam
Replies of Moslem faith I am.'

'The burden ye so gently bear,
Seems one that claims your utmost care,
And, doubtless, holds some precious freight,
My humble bark would gladly wait.'

'Thou speakest sooth; they skiff unmoor,
And waft us from the silent shore;
Nay, leave the sail still furled, and ply
The nearest oar that's scattered by,
And midway to those rocks where sleep
The channeled waters dark and deep.
Rest from your task - so - bravely done,
Of course had been right swiftly run;
Yet 'tis the longest voyage, I trow,
That one of -

Sullen it plunged, and slowly sank,
The calm wave rippled to the bank;
I watched it as it sank, methought
Some motion from the current caught
Bestirred it more, - 'twas but the beam
That checkered o'er the living stream:
I gazed, till vanishing from view,
Like lessening pebble it withdrew;
Still less and less, a speck of white
That gemmed the tide, then mocked the sight;
And all its hidden secrets sleep,
Known but to Genii of the deep,
Which, trembling in their coral caves,
They dare not whisper to the waves.

As rising on its purple wing
The insect-queen of eastern spring,
O'er emerald meadows of Kashmeer

Invites the young pursuer near,
And leads him on from flower to flower
A weary chase and wasted hour,
Then leaves him, as it soars on high,
With panting heart and tearful eye:
So beauty lures the full-grown child,
With hue as bright, and wing as wild:
A chase of idle hopes and fears,
Begun in folly, closed in tears.
If won, to equal ills betrayed,
Woe waits the insect and the maid;
A life of pain, the loss of peace,
From infant's play and man's caprice:
The lovely toy so fiercely sought
Hath lost its charm by being caught,
For every touch that wooed its stay
Hath brushed its brightest hues away,
Till charm, and hue, and beauty gone,
'Tis left to fly or fall alone.
With wounded wing, or bleeding breast,
Ah! Where shall either victim rest?
Can this with faded pinion soar
From rose to tulip as before?
Or beauty, blighted in an hour,
Find joy within her broken bower?
No: gayer insects fluttering by
Ne'er droop the wing o'er those that die,
And lovelier things have mercy shown
To every failing but their own,
And every woe a tear can claim
Except an erring sister's shame.

The mind that broods o'er guilty woes,
Is like the scorpion girt by fire;

In circle narrowing as it glows,
The flames around their captive close,
Till inly searched by thousand throes,
And maddening in her ire,
One sad and sole relief she knows,
The sting she nourished for her foes,
Whose venom never yet was vain,
Gives but one pang, and cures all pain,
So do the dark in soul expire,
Or live like scorpion girt by fire;
So writhes the mind remorse hath riven,
Unfit for earth, undoomed for heaven,
Darkness above, despair beneath,
Around it flame, within it death!

Black Hassan from the harem flies,
Nor bends on woman's form his eyes;
The unwonted chase each hour employs,
Yet shares he not the hunter's joys.
Not thus was Hassan wont to fly
When Leila dwelt in his Serai.
Doth Leila there no longer dwell?
That tale can only Hassan tell:

Strange rumours in our city say
Upon that eve she fled away
When Rhamazan's last sun was set,
And flashing from each minaret
Millions of lamps proclaimed the feast
Of Bairam through the boundless East.
'Twas then she went as to the bath,
Which Hassan vainly searched in wrath;
For she was flown her master's rage
In likeness of a Georgian page,

And far beyond the Moslem's power
Had wronged him with the faithless Giaour.
Somewhat of this had Hassan deemed;
But still so fond, so fair she seemed,
Too well he trusted to the slave
Whose treachery deserved a grave:
And on that eve had gone to mosque,
And thence to feast in his kiosk.
Such is the tale his Nubians tell,
Who did not watch their charge too well;
But others say, that on that night,
By pale Phingari's trembling light,
The Giaour upon his jet-black steed
Was seen, but seen alone to speed
With bloody spur along the shore,
Nor maid nor page behind him bore.

Her eye's dark charm 'twere vain to tell,
But gaze on that of the gazelle,
It will assist thy fancy well;
As large, as languishingly dark,
But soul beamed forth in every spark
That darted from beneath the lid,
Bright as the jewel of Giamschild.
Yea, Soul, and should our prophet say
That form was nought but breathing clay,
By Allah! I would answer nay;
Though on Al-Sirat's arch I stood,
Which totters o'er the fiery flood,
With Paradise within my view,
And all his Houris beckoning through.
Oh! Who young Leila's glance could read
And keep that portion of his creed,
Which saith that woman is but dust,

A soulless toy for tyrant's lust?
On her might Muftis might gaze, and own
That through her eye the Immortal shone;
On her fair cheek's unfading hue
The young pomegranate's blossoms strew
Their bloom in blushes ever new;
Her hair in hyacinthine flow,
When left to roll its folds below,
As midst her handmaids in the hall
She stood superior to them all,
Hath swept the marble where her feet
Gleamed whiter than the mountain sleet
Ere from the cloud that gave it birth
It fell, and caught one stain of earth.
The cygnet nobly walks the water;
So moved on earth Circassia's daughter,
The loveliest bird of Franguestan!
As rears her crest the ruffled swan,
And spurns the wave with wings of pride,
When pass the steps of stranger man
Along the banks that bound her tide;
Thus rose fair Leila's whiter neck:-
Thus armed with beauty would she check
Intrusion's glance, till folly's gaze
Shrunk from the charms it meant to praise:
Thus high and graceful as her gait;
Her heart as tender to her mate;
Her mate - stern Hassan, who was he?
Alas! That name was not for thee!

Stern Hassan hath a journey ta'en
With twenty vassals in his train,
Each armed, as best becomes a man,
With arquebuss and ataghan;

The chief before, as decked for war,
Bears in his belt the scimitar
Stain'd with the best of Arnaut blood
When in the pass the rebels stood,
And few returned to tell the tale
Of what befell in Parne's vale.
The pistols which his girdle bore
Were those that once a pasha wore,
Which still, though gemmed and bossed with gold,
Even robbers tremble to behold.
'Tis said he goes to woo a bride
More true than her who left his side;
The faithless slave that broke her bower,
And - worse than faithless - for a Giaour!

The sun's last rays are on the hill,
And sparkle in the fountain rill,
Whose welcome waters, cool and clear,
Draw blessings from the mountaineer:
Here may the loitering merchant Greek
Find that repose 'twere vain to seek
In cities lodged too near his lord,
And trembling for his secret hoard -
Here may he rest where none can see,
In crowds a slave, in deserts free;
And with forbidden wine may stain
The bowl a Moslem must not drain.

The foremost Tartar's in the gap,
Conspicuous by his yellow cap;
The rest in lengthening line the while
Wind slowly through the long defile:
Above, the mountain rears a peak,
Where vultures whet the thirsty beak,

And theirs may be a feast tonight,
Shall tempt them down ere morrow's light;
Beneath, a river's wintry stream
Has shrunk before the summer beam,
And left a channel bleak and bare,
Save shrubs that spring to perish there:
Each side the midway path there lay
Small broken crags of granite grey
By time, or mountain lightning, riven
From summits clad in mists of heaven;
For where is he that hath beheld
The peak of Liakura unveiled?

They reach the grove of pine at last:
'Bismillah! now the peril's past;
For yonder view the opening plain,
And there we'll prick our steeds amain.'
The Chiaus spake, and as he said,
A bullet whistled o'er his head;
The foremost Tartar bites the ground!
Scarce had they time to check the rein,
Swift from their steeds the riders bound;
But three shall never mount again:
Unseen the foes that gave the wound,
The dying ask revenge in vain.
With steel unsheathed, and carbine bent,
Some o'er their courser's harness leant,
Half sheltered by the steed;
Some fly behind the nearest rock,
And there await the coming shock,
Nor tamely stand to bleed
Beneath the shaft of foes unseen,
Who dare not quit their craggy screen.
Stern Hassan only from his horse

Disdains to light, and keeps his course,
Till fiery flashes in the van
Proclaim too sure the robber-clan
Have well secured the only way
Could now avail the promised prey;
Then curled his very beard with ire,
And glared his eye with fiercer fire:
'Though far and near the bullets hiss,
I've 'scaped a bloodier hour than this.'
And now the foe their covert quit,
And call his vassals to submit;
But Hassan's frown and furious word
Are dreaded more than hostile sword,
Nor of his little band a man
Resigned carbine or ataghan,
Nor raised the craven cry, Amaun!
In fuller sight, more near and near,
The lately ambushed foes appear,
And, issuing from the grove, advance
Some who on battle-charger prance.
Who leads them on with foreign brand,
Far flashing in his red right hand?
"Tis he! 'tis he! I know him now;
I know him by his pallid brow;
I know him by the evil eye
That aids his envious treachery;
I know him by his jet-black barb:
Though now arrayed in Arnaut garb
Apostate from his own vile faith,
It shall not save him from the death:
'Tis he! well met in any hour,
Lost Leila's love, accursed Giaour!

As rolls the river into ocean,

In sable torrent wildly streaming;
As the sea-tide's opposing motion,
In azure column Proudly gleaming
Beats back the current many a rood,
In curling foam and mingling flood,
While eddying whirl, and breaking wave,
Roused by the blast of winter, rave;
Through sparkling spray, in thundering clash,
The lightnings of the waters flash
In awful whiteness o'er the shore,
That shines and shakes beneath the roar;
Thus - as the stream, and Ocean greet,
With waves that madden as they meet -
Thus join the bands, whom mutual wrong,
And fate, and fury, drive along.
The bickering sabres' shivering jar;
And pealing wide or ringing near
Its echoes on the throbbing ear,
The deathshot hissing from afar;
The shock, the shout, the groan of war,
Reverberate along that vale
More suited to the shepherds tale:
Though few the numbers - theirs the strife
That neither spares nor speaks for life!
Ah! fondly youthful hearts can press,
To seize and share the dear caress;
But love itself could never pant
For all that beauty sighs to grant
With half the fervour hate bestows
Upon the last embrace of foes,
When grappling in the fight they fold
Those arms that ne'er shall lose their hold:
Friends meet to part; love laughs at faith;
True foes, once met, are joined till death!

With sabre shivered to the hilt,
Yet dripping with the blood he spilt;
Yet strained within the severed hand
Which quivers round that faithless brand;
His turban far behind him rolled,
And cleft in twain its firmest fold;
His flowing robe by falchion torn,
And crimson as those clouds of morn
That, streaked with dusky red, portend
The day shall have a stormy end;
A stain on every bush that bore
A fragment of his palampore
His breast with wounds unnumbered riven,
His back to earth, his face to heaven,
Fallen Hassan lies - his unclosed eye
Yet lowering on his enemy,
As if the hour that sealed his fate
Surviving left his quenchless hate;
And o'er him bends that foe with brow
As dark as his that bled below.

'Yes, Leila sleeps beneath the wave,
But his shall be a redder grave;
Her spirit pointed well the steel
Which taught that felon heart to feel.
He called the Prophet, but his power
Was vain against the vengeful Giaour:
He called on Allah - but the word.
Arose unheeded or unheard.
Thou Paynim fool! could Leila's prayer
Be passed, and thine accorded there?
I watched my time, I leagued with these,
The traitor in his turn to seize;

My wrath is wreaked, the deed is done,
And now I go - but go alone.'

The browsing camels' bells are tinkling:
His mother looked from her lattice high -
She saw the dews of eve besprinkling
The pasture green beneath her eye,
She saw the planets faintly twinkling:
Tis twilight - sure his train is nigh.'
She could not rest in the garden-bower,
But gazed through the grate of his steepest tower:
'Why comes he not? his steeds are fleet,
Nor shrink they from the summer heat;
Why sends not the bridegroom his promised gift?
Is his heart more cold, or his barb less swift?
Oh, false reproach! yon Tartar now
Has gained our nearest mountain's brow,
And warily the steep descends,
And now within the valley bends;
And he bears the gift at his saddle bow
How could I deem his courser slow?
Right well my largess shall repay
His welcome speed, and weary way.'
The Tartar lighted at the gate,
But scarce upheld his fainting weight!
His swarthy visage spake distress,
But this might be from weariness;
His garb with sanguine spots was dyed,
But these might be from his courser's side;
He drew the token from his vest -
Angel of Death! 'tis Hassan's cloven crest!
His calpac rent - his caftan red -
'Lady, a fearful bride thy son hath wed:
Me, not from mercy, did they spare,

But this empurpled pledge to bear.
Peace to the brave! whose blood is spilt:
Woe to the Giaour! for his the guilt.'

A turban carved in coarsest stone,
A pillar with rank weeds o'ergrown,
Whereon can now be scarcely read
The Koran verse that mourns the dead,
Point out the spot where Hassan fell
A victim in that lonely dell.
There sleeps as true an Osmanlie
As e'er at Mecca bent the knee;
As ever scorned forbidden wine,
Or prayed with face towards the shrine,
In orisons resumed anew
At solemn sound of 'Allah Hu!'
Yet died he by a stranger's hand,
And stranger in his native land;
Yet died he as in arms he stood,
And unavenged, at least in blood.
But him the maids of Paradise
Impatient to their halls invite,
And the dark Heaven of Houris' eyes
On him shall glance for ever bright;
They come - their kerchiefs green they wave,
And welcome with a kiss the brave!
Who falls in battle 'gainst a Giaour
Is worthiest an immortal bower.

But thou, false Infidel! shalt writhe
Beneath avenging Monkir's scythe;
And from its torment 'scape alone
To wander round lost Eblis' throne;
And fire unquenched, unquenchable,

Around, within, thy heart shall dwell;
Nor ear can hear nor tongue can tell
The tortures of that inward hell!
But first, on earth as vampire sent,
Thy corse shall from its tomb be rent:
Then ghastly haunt thy native place,
And suck the blood of all thy race;
There from thy daughter, sister, wife,
At midnight drain the stream of life;
Yet loathe the banquet which perforce
Must feed thy livid living corse:
Thy victims ere they yet expire
Shall know the demon for their sire,
As cursing thee, thou cursing them,
Thy flowers are withered on the stem.
But one that for thy crime must fall,
The youngest, most beloved of all,
Shall bless thee with a father's name -
That word shall wrap thy heart in flame!
Yet must thou end thy task, and mark
Her cheek's last tinge, her eye's last spark,
And the last glassy glance must view
Which freezes o'er its lifeless blue;
Then with unhallowed hand shalt tear
The tresses of her yellow hair,
Of which in life a lock when shorn
Affection's fondest pledge was worn,
But now is borne away by thee,
Memorial of thine agony!
Wet with thine own best blood shall drip
Thy gnashing tooth and haggard lip;
Then stalking to thy sullen grave,
Go - and with Gouls and Afrits rave;
Till these in horror shrink away

From spectre more accursed than they!

'How name ye yon lone Caloyer?
His features I have scanned before
In mine own land: 'tis many a year,
Since, dashing by the lonely shore,
I saw him urge as fleet a steed
As ever served a horseman's need.
But once I saw that face, yet then
It was so marked with inward pain,
I could not pass it by again;
It breathes the same dark spirit now,
As death were stamped upon his brow.

Tis twice three years at summer tide
Since first among our freres he came;
And here it soothes him to abide
For some dark deed he will not name.
But never at our vesper prayer,
Nor e'er before confession chair
Kneels he, nor recks he when arise
Incense or anthem to the skies,
But broods within his cell alone,
His faith and race alike unknown.
The sea from Paynim land he crost,
And here ascended from the coast;
Yet seems he not of Othman race,
But only Christian in his face:
I'd judge him some stray renegade,
Repentant of the change he made,
Save that he shuns our holy shrine,
Nor tastes the sacred bread and wine.
Great largess to these walls he brought,
And thus our abbot's favour bought;

But were I prior, not a day
Should brook such stranger's further stay,
Or pent within our penance cell
Should doom him there for aye to dwell.
Much in his visions mutters he
Of maiden whelmed beneath the sea;
Of sabres clashing, foemen flying,
Wrongs avenged, and Moslem dying.
On cliff he hath been known to stand,
And rave as to some bloody hand
Fresh severed from its parent limb,
Invisible to all but him,
Which beckons onward to his grave,
And lures to leap into the wave.'

Dark and unearthly is the scowl
That glares beneath his dusky cowl:
The flash of that dilating eye
Reveals too much of times gone by;
Though varying, indistinct its hue,
Oft will his glance the gazer rue,
For in it lurks that nameless spell,
Which speaks, itself unspeakable,
A spirit yet unquelled and high,
That claims and keeps ascendency;
And like the bird whose pinions quake,
But cannot fly the gazing snake,
Will others quail beneath his look,
Nor 'scape the glance they scarce can brook.
From him the half-affrighted friar
When met alone would fain retire,
As if that eye and bitter smile
Transferred to others fear and guile:
Not oft to smile descendeth he,

And when he doth 'tis sad to see
That he but mocks at misery.
How that pale lip will curl and quiver!
Then fix once more as if for ever;
As if his sorrow or disdain
Forbade him e'er to smile again.
Well were it so - such ghastly mirth
From joyaunce ne'er derived its birth.
But sadder still it were to trace
What once were feelings in that face:
Time hath not yet the features fixed,
But brighter traits with evil mixed;
And there are hues not always faded,
Which speak a mind not all degraded
Even by the crimes through which it waded:
The common crowd but see the gloom
Of wayward deeds, and fitting doom;
The close observer can espy
A noble soul, and lineage high:
Alas! though both bestowed in vain,
Which grief could change, and guilt could stain,
It was no vulgar tenement
To which such lofty gifts were lent,
And still with little less than dread
On such the sight is riveted.
The roofless cot, decayed and rent,
Will scarce delay the passer-by;
The tower by war or tempest bent,
While yet may frown one battlement,
Demands and daunts the stranger's eye;
Each ivied arch, and pillar lone,
Pleads haughtily for glories gone!

'His floating robe around him folding,

Slow sweeps he through the columned aisle;
With dread beheld, with gloom beholding
The rites that sanctify the pile.
But when the anthem shakes the choir,
And kneel the monks, his steps retire;
By yonder lone and wavering torch
His aspect glares within the porch;
There will he pause till all is done -
And hear the prayer, but utter none.
See - by the half-illumined wall
His hood fly back, his dark hair fall,
That pale brow wildly wreathing round,
As if the Gorgon there had bound
The sablest of the serpent-braid
That o'er her fearful forehead strayed:
For he declines the convent oath
And leaves those locks unhallowed growth,
But wears our garb in all beside;
And, not from piety but pride,
Gives wealth to walls that never heard
Of his one holy vow nor word.
Lo! - mark ye, as the harmony
Peals louder praises to the sky,
That livid cheek, that stony air
Of mixed defiance and despair!
Saint Francis, keep him from the shrine!
Else may we dread the wrath divine
Made manifest by awful sign.
If ever evil angel bore
The form of mortal, such he wore:
By all my hope of sins forgiven,
Such looks are not of earth nor heaven!'

To love the softest hearts are prone,

But such can ne'er be all his own;
Too timid in his woes to share,
Too meek to meet, or brave despair;
And sterner hearts alone may feel
The wound that time can never heal.
The rugged metal of the mine,
Must burn before its surface shine,
But plunged within the furnace-flame,
It bends and melts - though still the same;
Then tempered to thy want, or will,
'Twill serve thee to defend or kill;
A breast-plate for thine hour of need,
Or blade to bid thy foeman bleed;
But if a dagger's form it bear,
Let those who shape its edge, beware!
Thus passion's fire, and woman's art,
Can turn and tame the sterner heart;
From these its form and tone are ta'en,
And what they make it, must remain,
But break - before it bend again.

If solitude succeed to grief,
  Release from pain is slight relief;
  The vacant bosom's wilderness
  Might thank the pang that made it less.
  We loathe what none are left to share:
  Even bliss - 'twere woe alone to bear;
  The heart once left thus desolate
  Must fly at last for ease - to hate.
  It is as if the dead could feel
  The icy worm around them steal,
  And shudder, as the reptiles creep
  To revel o'er their rotting sleep,
  Without the power to scare away

The cold consumers of their clay I
It is as if the desert-bird,
Whose beak unlocks her bosom's stream
To still her famished nestlings' scream,
Nor mourns a life to them transferred,
Should rend her rash devoted breast,
And find them flown her empty nest.
The keenest pangs the wretched find
Are rapture to the dreary void,
The leafless desert of the mind,
The waste of feelings unemployed.
Who would be doomed to gaze upon
A sky without a cloud or sun?
Less hideous far the tempest's roar
Than ne'er to brave the billows more -
Thrown, when the war of winds is o'er,
A lonely wreck on fortune's shore,
'Mid sullen calm, and silent bay,
Unseen to drop by dull decay; -
Better to sink beneath the shock
Than moulder piecemeal on the rock!

'Father! thy days have passed in peace,
'Mid counted beads, and countless prayer;
To bid the sins of others cease
Thyself without a crime or care,
Save transient ills that all must bear,
Has been thy lot from youth to age;
And thou wilt bless thee from the rage
Of passions fierce and uncontrolled,
Such as thy penitents unfold,
Whose secret sins and sorrows rest
Within thy pure and pitying breast.
My days, though few, have passed below

In much of joy, but more of woe;
Yet still in hours of love or strife,
I've 'scaped the weariness of life:
Now leagued with friends, now girt by foes,
I loathed the languor of repose.
Now nothing left to love or hate,
No more with hope or pride elate,
I'd rather be the thing that crawls
Most noxious o'er a dungeon's walls,
Than pass my dull, unvarying days,
Condemned to meditate and gaze.
Yet, lurks a wish within my breast
For rest - but not to feel 'tis rest
Soon shall my fate that wish fulfil;
And I shall sleep without the dream
Of what I was, and would be still,
Dark as to thee my deeds may seem:
My memory now is but the tomb
Of joys long dead; my hope, their doom:
Though better to have died with those
Than bear a life of lingering woes.
My spirit shrunk not to sustain
The searching throes of ceaseless pain;
Nor sought the self-accorded grave
Of ancient fool and modern knave:
Yet death I have not feared to meet;
And the field it had been sweet,
Had danger wooed me on to move
The slave of glory, not of love.
I've braved it - not for honour's boast;
I smile at laurels won or lost;
To such let others carve their way,
For high renown, or hireling pay:
But place again before my eyes

Aught that I deem a worthy prize
The maid I love, the man I hate,
And I will hunt the steps of fate,
To save or slay, as these require,
Through rending steel, and rolling fire:
Nor needest thou doubt this speech from one
Who would but do ~ what he hath done.
Death is but what the haughty brave,
The weak must bear, the wretch must crave;
Then let life go to him who gave:
I have not quailed to danger's brow
When high and happy - need I now?

'I loved her, Friar! nay, adored -
But these are words that all can use -
I proved it more in deed than word;
There's blood upon that dinted sword,
A stain its steel can never lose:
'Twas shed for her, who died for me,
It warmed the heart of one abhorred:
Nay, start not - no - nor bend thy knee,
Nor midst my sins such act record;
Thou wilt absolve me from the deed,
For he was hostile to thy creed!
The very name of Nazarene
Was wormwood to his Paynim spleen.
Ungrateful fool! since but for brands
Well wielded in some hardy hands,
And wounds by Galileans given -
The surest pass to Turkish heaven
For him his Houris still might wait
Impatient at the Prophet's gate.
I loved her - love will find its way
Through paths where wolves would fear to prey;

And if it dares enough, 'twere hard
If passion met not some reward -
No matter how, or where, or why,
I did not vainly seek, nor sigh:
Yet sometimes, with remorse, in vain
I wish she had not loved again.
She died - I dare not tell thee how;
But look - 'tis written on my brow!
There read of Cain the curse and crime,
In characters unworn by time:
Still, ere thou dost condemn me, pause;
Not mine the act, though I the cause.
Yet did he but what I had done
Had she been false to more than one.
Faithless to him, he gave the blow;
But true to me, I laid him low:
Howe'er deserved her doom might be,
Her treachery was truth to me;
To me she gave her heart, that all
Which tyranny can ne'er enthral;
And I, alas! too late to save!
Yet all I then could give, I gave,
'Twas some relief, our foe a grave.
His death sits lightly; but her fate
Has made me - what thou well mayest hate.
His doom was sealed - he knew it well
Warned by the voice of stern Taheer,
Deep in whose darkly boding ear
The deathshot pealed of murder near,
As filed the troop to where they fell!
He died too in the battle broil,
A time that heeds nor pain nor toil;
One cry to Mahomet for aid,
One prayer to Allah all he made:

He knew and crossed me in the fray -
I gazed upon him where he lay,
And watched his spirit ebb away:
Though pierced like pard by hunters' steel,
He felt not half that now I feel.
I searched, but vainly searched, to find
The workings of a wounded mind;
Each feature of that sullen corse
Betrayed his rage, but no remorse.
Oh, what had vengeance given to trace
Despair upon his dying face I
The late repentance of that hour,
When penitence hath lost her power
To tear one terror from the grave,
And will not soothe, and cannot save.

'The cold in clime are cold in blood,
Their love can scarce deserve the name;
But mine was like a lava flood
That boils in Etna's breast of flame.
I cannot prate in puling strain
Of ladye-love, and beauty's chain:
If changing cheek, and searching vein,
Lips taught to writhe, but not complain,
If bursting heart, and maddening brain,
And daring deed, and vengeful steel,
And all that I have felt, and feel,
Betoken love - that love was mine,
And shown by many a bitter sign.
'Tis true, I could not whine nor sigh,
I knew but to obtain or die.
I die - but first I have possessed,
And come what may, I have been blessed.
Shall I the doom I sought upbraid?

No - reft of all, yet undismayed
But for the thought of Leila slain,
Give me the pleasure with the pain,
So would I live and love again.
I grieve, but not, my holy guide!
For him who dies, but her who died:
She sleeps beneath the wandering wave
Ah! had she but an earthly grave,
This breaking heart and throbbing head
Should seek and share her narrow bed.
She was a form of life and light,
That, seen, became a part of sight;
And rose, where'er I turned mine eye,
The morning-star of memory!

'Yes, love indeed is light from heaven..
A spark of that immortal fire
With angels shared, by Allah given,
To lift from earth our low desire.
Devotion wafts the mind above,
But Heaven itself descends in love;
A feeling from the Godhead caught,
To wean from self each sordid thought;
A ray of him who formed the whole;
A glory circling round the soul !
I grant my love imperfect, all
That mortals by the name miscall;
Then deem it evil, what thou wilt;
But say, oh say, hers was not guilt !
She was my life's unerring light:
That quenched, what beam shall break my night?
Oh! would it shone to lead me still,
Although to death or deadliest ill!
Why marvel ye, if they who lose

This present joy, this future hope,
No more with sorrow meekly cope;
In phrensy then their fate accuse;
In madness do those fearful deeds
That seem to add but guilt to woe?
Alas! the breast that inly bleeds
Hath nought to dread from outward blow;
Who falls from all he knows of bliss,
Cares little into what abyss.
Fierce as the gloomy vulture's now
To thee, old man, my deeds appear:
I read abhorrence on thy brow,
And this too was I born to bear!
'Tis true, that, like that bird of prey,
With havock have I marked my way:
But this was taught me by the dove,
To die - and know no second love.
This lesson yet hath man to learn,
Taught by the thing he dares to spurn:
The bird that sings within the brake,
The swan that swims upon the lake,
One mate, and one alone, will take.
And let the fool still prone to range,
And sneer on all who cannot change,
Partake his jest with boasting boys;
I envy not his varied joys,
But deem such feeble, heartless man,
Less than yon solitary swan;
Far, far beneath the shallow maid
He left believing and betrayed.
Such shame at least was never mine -
Leila! each thought was only thine!
My good, my guilt, my weal, my woe,
My hope on high - my all below.

Earth holds no other like to thee,
Or, if it doth, in vain for me:
For worlds I dare not view the dame
Resembling thee, yet not the same.
The very crimes that mar my youth,
This bed of death - attest my truth!
'Tis all too late - thou wert, thou art
The cherished madness of my heart!

'And she was lost - and yet I breathed,
But not the breath of human life:
A serpent round my heart was wreathed,
And stung my every thought to strife.
Alike all time, abhorred all place,
Shuddering I shrunk from Nature's face,
Where every hue that charmed before
The blackness of my bosom wore.
The rest thou dost already know,
And all my sins, and half my woe.
But talk no more of penitence;
Thou see'st I soon shall part from hence:
And if thy holy tale were true,
The deed that's done canst thou undo?
Think me not thankless - but this grief
Looks not to priesthood for relief.
My soul's estate in secret guess:
But wouldst thou pity more, say less.
When thou canst bid my Leila live,
Then will I sue thee to forgive;
Then plead my cause in that high place
Where purchased masses proffer grace.
Go, when the hunter's hand hath wrung
From forest-cave her shrieking young,
And calm the lonely lioness:

But soothe not - mock not my distress!

'In earlier days, and calmer hours,
When heart with heart delights to blend,
Where bloom my native valley's bowers
I had - Ah! have I now? - a friend!
To him this pledge I charge thee send,
Memorial of a youthful vow;
I would remind him of my end:
Though souls absorbed like mine allow
Brief thought to distant friendship's claim,
Yet dear to him my blighted name.
'Tis strange - he prophesied my doom,
And I have smiled - I then could smile -
When prudence would his voice assume,
And warn - I recked not what - the while:
But now remembrance whispers o'er
Those accents scarcely marked before.
Say - that his bodings came to pass,
And he will start to hear their truth,
And wish his words had not been sooth:
Tell him, unheeding as I was,
Through many a busy bitter scene
Of all our golden youth had been,
In pain, my faltering tongue had tried
To bless his memory ere I died;
But Heaven in wrath would turn away,
If guilt should for the guiltless pray.
I do not ask him not to blame,
Too gentle he to wound my name;
And what have I to do with fame?
I do not ask him not to mourn,
Such cold request might sound like scorn;
And what than friendship's manly tear

May better grace a brother's bier?
But bear this ring, his own of old,
And tell him - what thou dost behold!
The withered frame, the ruined mind,
The wrack by passion left behind,
A shrivelled scroll, a scattered leaf,
Seared by the autumn blast of grief!

'Tell me no more of fancy's gleam,
No, father, no, 'twas not a dream;
Alas! the dreamer first must sleep.
I only watched, and wished to weep;
But could not, for my burning brow
Throbbed to the very brain as now:
I wished but for a single tear,
As something welcome, new, and dear-;
I wished it then, I wish it still;
Despair is stronger than my will.
Waste not thine orison, despair
Is mightier than thy pious prayer:
I would not if I might, be blest;
I want no paradise, but rest.
'Twas then, I tell thee, father! then
I saw her; yes, she lived again;
And shining in her white symar,
As through yon pale grey cloud the star
Which now I gaze on, as on her,
Who looked and looks far lovelier;
Dimly I view its trembling spark;
Tomorrow's night shall be more dark;
And I, before its rays appear,
That lifeless thing the living fear.
I wander, father! for my soul
Is fleeting towards the final goal.

I saw her, friar! and I rose
Forgetful of our former woes;
And rushing from my couch, I dart,
And clasp her to my desperate heart;
I clasp - what is it that I clasp?
No breathing form within my grasp,
No heart that beats reply to mine,
Yet, Leila! yet the form is thine!
And art thou, dearest, changed so much,
As meet my eye, yet mock my touch?
Ah! were thy beauties e'er so cold,
I care not; so my arms enfold
The all they ever wished to hold.
Alas! around a shadow prest,
They shrink upon my lonely breast;
Yet still 'tis there! In silence stands,
And beckons with beseeching hands!
With braided hair, and bright black eye -
I knew 'twas false - she could not die!
But he is dead! within the dell
I saw him buried where he fell;
He comes not, for he cannot break
From earth; why then art thou awake?
They told me wild waves rolled above
The face I view, the form I love;
They told me - 'twas a hideous tale I
I'd tell it, but my tongue would fail:
If true, and from thine ocean-cave
Thou com'st to claim a calmer grave;
Oh! pass thy dewy fingers o'er
This brow that then will burn no more;
Or place them on my hopeless heart:
But, shape or shade! whate'er thou art,
In mercy ne'er again depart!

Or farther with thee bear my soul
Than winds can waft or waters roll!

'Such is my name, and such my tale.
Confessor ! to thy secret ear
I breathe the sorrows I bewail,
And thank thee for the generous tear
This glazing eye could never shed.
Then lay me with the humblest dead,
And, save the cross above my head,
Be neither name nor emblem spread,
By prying stranger to be read,
Or stay the passing pilgrims tread.'

He passed - nor of his name and race
Hath left a token or a trace,
Save what the father must not say
Who shrived him on his dying day:
This broken tale was all we knew
Of her he loved, or him he slew.